To: ~~Mum~~ Clae

From: Mum

365
Days

with
Winnie-the-Pooh

EGMONT

We bring stories to life

First published in 2006 by Egmont UK Ltd
239 Kensington High Street, London W8 6SA

Selected text from *WINNIE-THE-POOH, THE HOUSE AT POOH CORNER,*
WHEN WE WERE VERY YOUNG and *NOW WE ARE SIX* by A. A. Milne
© The Trustees of the Pooh Properties

Line drawings for *WINNIE-THE-POOH* and *THE HOUSE AT POOH CORNER,* © E.H. Shepard,
colouring © 1970, 1973 and 1974 E.H. Shepard and Egmont UK Ltd

Line drawings for *WHEN WE WERE VERY YOUNG* and *NOW WE ARE SIX* © E.H. Shepard,
colouring by Mark Burgess © 1989 Egmont UK Ltd

Sketches from *THE POOH SKETCHBOOK* © 1982 Lloyds TSB Bank PLC
Executors of the Estate of E.H. Shepard, and the E.H. Shepard Trust

This edition © 2006 The Trustees of the Pooh Properties
Book design © 2006 Egmont UK Ltd

ISBN 1 4052 2463 0
ISBN 978 1 4052 2463 5
1 3 5 7 9 10 8 6 4 2

Printed and bound in Singapore

A.A.MILNE

365
Days

with
Winnie-the-Pooh

EGMONT

January 1

One fine winter's day when Piglet was brushing away the snow in front of his house, he happened to look up, and there was Winnie-the-Pooh.

January 2

'Tracks,' said Piglet. 'Paw-marks.'
He gave a little squeak of excitement.
'Oh, Pooh! Do you think
it's a – a – a Woozle?'

January 3

'*What?*' said Piglet, with a jump.
And then, to show that he hadn't been
frightened, he jumped up and down
once or twice more in an
exercising sort of way.

January 4

'It is either Two Woozles and one, as it might be, Wizzle, or Two, as it might be, Wizzles and one, if so it is, Woozle.'

January 5

So they went on, feeling just a little anxious now, in case the three animals in front of them were of Hostile Intent.

January 6

Winnie-the-Pooh stopped again, and licked the tip
of his nose in a cooling manner, for he was feeling
more hot and anxious than ever in his life before.
There were four animals in front of them!

January 7

Christopher Robin came slowly down his tree.
'Silly old Bear,' he said, 'what *were* you doing?
First you went round the spinney twice by yourself, and then
Piglet ran after you and you went round again together . . .'

January 8

'I see now,' said Winnie-the-Pooh.
'I have been Foolish and Deluded,'
said he, 'and I am a Bear of
No Brain at All.'

January 9

'You're the Best Bear in All the
World,' said Christopher Robin soothingly.
'Am I?' said Pooh hopefully.

January 10

'I'm Tigger,' said Tigger.
'Oh!' said Pooh, for he had never
seen an animal like this before.

January 11

'Do Tiggers like honey?'
'They like everything,'
said Tigger cheerfully.

January 12

'Hallo!' said Pooh.

'Hallo!' said Tigger.

'I've found somebody just like me.
I thought I was the only one of them.'

January 13

'Tiggers don't like honey.'
'Oh!' said Pooh, and tried to make it
sound Sad and Regretful.

January 14

'I thought they liked everything.'
'Everything except honey,'
said Tigger.

January 15

Pooh felt rather pleased . . . and said that . . .
he would take Tigger round to Piglet's house,
and Tigger could try some of Piglet's haycorns.
'Thank you, Pooh,' said Tigger, 'because haycorns
is really what Tiggers like best.'

January 16

'Hallo, Piglet. This is Tigger.'
'Oh, is it?' said Piglet, and he edged
round to the other side of the table.
'I thought Tiggers were smaller than that.'
'Not the big ones,' said Tigger.

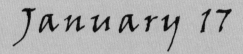

January 17

'Tiggers don't like haycorns.'
'But you said they liked everything
except honey,' said Pooh.
'Everything except honey *and* haycorns,'
explained Tigger.

January 18

Piglet, who was rather glad that
Tiggers didn't like haycorns, said,
'What about thistles?'
'Thistles,' said Tigger, 'is what
Tiggers like best.'

January 19

Eeyore led the way to the most
thistly looking patch of thistles
that ever was, and waved a hoof at it.
'A little patch I was keeping for
my birthday,' he said.

January 20

'*Ow!*' said Tigger.
'Your friend,' said Eeyore,
'appears to have bitten on a bee.'
Pooh's friend stopped shaking his head
to get the prickles out, and explained
that Tiggers didn't like thistles.

January 21

'What shall we do
about poor little Tigger?
If he never eats nothing
he'll never get bigger.'

January 22

'What is it?' whispered
Tigger to Piglet.
'His Strengthening Medicine,'
said Piglet. 'He hates it.'

January 23

Tigger came closer . . . the Extract of Malt had gone . . .
'He's taken my medicine, he's taken
my medicine, he's taken my medicine!'
sang Roo happily, thinking it was
a tremendous joke.

January 24

Which explains why he always lived at Kanga's house afterwards, and had Extract of Malt for breakfast, dinner and tea.

January 25

The Old Grey Donkey, Eeyore, stood by himself in a thistly corner of the Forest, his front feet well apart, his head on one side, and thought about things.

January 26

Sometimes he thought sadly to himself, 'Why?' and sometimes
he thought, 'Wherefore?' and sometimes he thought,
'Inasmuch as which?' – and sometimes he didn't quite
know what he *was* thinking about.

January 27

'And how are you?'
said Winnie-the-Pooh.
Eeyore shook his head
from side to side.
'Not very how,' he said.
'I don't seem to have felt at all
how for a long time.'

January 28

'Why, what's happened to your tail?'
he said in surprise.
'What *has* happened to it?' said Eeyore.
'It isn't there!'
'Are you sure?'

January 29

'Well, either a tail *is* there or it isn't there.
You can't make a mistake about it,
and yours *isn't* there!'

January 30

'That Accounts for a Good Deal,'
said Eeyore gloomily. 'It Explains Everything.
No Wonder.'

January 31

'Eeyore,' he said solemnly,
'I, Winnie-the-Pooh, will
find your tail for you.'

February 1

Owl lived at The Chestnuts, an old-world residence of great charm, which was grander than anybody else's, or seemed so to Bear, because it had both a knocker *and* a bell-pull.

Underneath the knocker there was a notice which said:
PLES RING IF AN RNSER IS REQIRD.
Underneath the bell-pull there was a notice which said:
PLEZ CNOKE IF AN RNSR IS NOT REQID.

February 3

'Hallo, Pooh,' he said. 'How's things?'
'Terrible and Sad,' said Pooh, 'because Eeyore,
who is a friend of mine, has lost his tail.'

February 4

'Well,' said Owl,
'the customary
procedure in such
cases is as follows.'

February 5

'What does Crustimoney
Proseedcake mean?' said Pooh.

'Handsome bell-rope,
isn't it?' said Owl.
Pooh nodded.
'It reminds me of
something,' he said,
'but I can't think what.'

February 7

'My dear friend, Eeyore.
He was – he was
fond of it.'
'Fond of it?'
'Attached to it,' said
Winnie-the-Pooh sadly.

February 8

. . . when Christopher Robin had nailed it
on in its right place again, Eeyore frisked
about the forest, waving his tail . . .

February 9

'*Who found the Tail?*
"I," said Pooh,
"At a quarter to two
(Only it was quarter to eleven really),
I found the Tail!"'

February 10

It was just the day for Organizing Something,
or for Writing a Notice Signed Rabbit,
or for Seeing What Everybody Else Thought About It.

February 11

Gon out
Backson
Bisy
Backson
C.R.

'Ha!' said Rabbit, feeling quite happy again.

'Another notice!'

This is what it said:

February 12

Owl looked at the notice again. To one of his education
the reading of it was easy. 'Gon out,
Backson. Bisy, Backson' – just the sort
of thing you'd expect to see on a notice.

February 13

'Christopher Robin has gone out somewhere with Backson. He and Backson are busy together. Have you seen a Backson anywhere about in the Forest lately?'

February 14

'Well, the point is, have you seen a Spotted
or Herbaceous Backson in the Forest, at all?'
'No,' said Pooh. 'Not a – no,' said Pooh.
'I saw Tigger just now.'
'That's no good.'

February 15

'What would *you* do, if *your* house was blown down?'
Before Piglet could think, Pooh answered for him.
'He'd come and live with me,' said Pooh, 'wouldn't you, Piglet?'
Piglet squeezed his paw. 'Thank you, Pooh,' he said, 'I should love to.'

February 16

'We had breakfast
together yesterday.
By the Pine Trees.
I'd made up a
little basket,
just a little, fair-sized
basket, an ordinary biggish
sort of basket, full of –'

February 17

So he hurried out again, saying to himself,
'Eeyore, Violets,' and then,
'Violets, Eeyore,'
in case he forgot . . .

February 18

'Do you know what A means, little Piglet?'
'No, Eeyore, I don't.'
'It means Learning, it means Education,
it means all the things that you and Pooh
haven't got. That's what A means.'

February 19

'An A,' said Rabbit,
'but not a very good one.'

February 20

'What does Christopher Robin do in the mornings?
He learns. He becomes Educated. He instigorates –
I *think* that is the word he mentioned.'

February 21

At first Pooh and Rabbit and Piglet walked together,
and Tigger ran round them in circles, and then,
when the path got narrower, Rabbit, Piglet and Pooh
walked one after another, and Tigger ran round
them in oblongs . . .

February 22

And as they got higher, the mist got thicker, so that Tigger kept disappearing, and then when you thought he wasn't there, there he was again, saying, 'I say, come on,' and before you could say anything, there he wasn't.

February 23

Piglet sidled up to Pooh from behind.

'Pooh!' he whispered.

'Yes, Piglet?'

'Nothing,' said Piglet, taking Pooh's paw.

'I just wanted to be sure of you.'

February 24

And the
Small and Sorry Rabbit
rushed through the mist
at the noise, and it
suddenly turned into
Tigger . . .

February 25

'Aha!' said Pooh. *(Rum-tum-tiddle-um-tum.)* 'If I know anything about anything, that hole means Rabbit,' he said, 'and Rabbit means Company,' he said . . .

So he bent down, put his head into the hole, and called out: 'Is anybody at home?'

February 26

'No!' said a voice; and then added,
'You needn't shout so loud.
I heard you quite well the first time.'

February 27

'Well, could you very kindly tell me where Rabbit is?'
'He has gone to see his friend Pooh Bear,
who is a great friend of his.'
'But this *is* Me!' said Bear, very much surprised.
'What sort of Me?'
'Pooh Bear.'

February 28
(and perhaps February 29)

'It may be,' said Pooh.
'Sometimes it is, and
sometimes it isn't.'

March 1

Pooh always liked a little
something at eleven o'clock
in the morning . . . and
when Rabbit said,
'Honey or condensed milk
with your bread?'
he was so excited that he said,
'Both,' and then, so as not
to seem greedy, he added,
'But don't bother about
the bread, please.'

March 2

And for a long time after
that he said nothing . . .
until at last, humming to himself
in a rather sticky voice, he got up,
shook Rabbit lovingly by the paw,
and said that he must be going on.
'Must you?' said Rabbit politely.

March 3

'Oh, help!' said Pooh. 'I'd better go back.'

'Oh, bother!' said Pooh. 'I shall have to go on.'

'I can't do either!' said Pooh.

'Oh, help *and* bother!'

March 4

'The fact is,'
said Rabbit,
'you're stuck.'
'It all comes,'
said Pooh crossly,
'of not having
front doors big enough.'
'It all comes,'
said Rabbit sternly,
'of eating too much.'

March 5

'How long does getting thin take?'
asked Pooh anxiously.
'About a week,
I should think.'
'But I can't stay here
for a *week*!'
'You can *stay* here all right,
silly old Bear.
It's getting you out which
is so difficult.'

March 6

'Then would you read a Sustaining Book, such as would help and comfort a Wedged Bear in Great Tightness?'

March 7

... they all pulled together ...
And for a long time Pooh only said
'*Ow!*' ... And '*Oh!*' ...
And then, all of a sudden, he said '*Pop!*'
just as if a cork were
coming out of a bottle.

March 8

'Cottleston, Cottleston, Cottleston Pie,
Why does a chicken, I don't know why.
Ask me a riddle and I reply:
"Cottleston, Cottleston, Cottleston Pie."'

March 9

'Cottleston, Cottleston, Cottleston Pie,
A fly can't bird, but a bird can fly.
Ask me a riddle and I reply:
"Cottleston, Cottleston, Cottleston Pie."'

March 10

'I know I had a jar
of honey there.
A full jar, full of honey
right up to the top,
and it had HUNNY
written on it, so that
I should know it was honey.'

March 11

. . . he found a small tin of condensed milk, and something seemed to tell him that Tiggers didn't like this, so he took it into a corner by itself, and went with it to see that nobody interrupted it.

March 12

As he got nearer to it his nose told him that it
was indeed honey, and his tongue came out and
began to polish up his mouth, ready for it.

March 13

'Bother!' said Pooh, as he got his nose inside the jar. 'A Heffalump has been eating it!' And then he thought a little and said, 'Oh, no, *I* did. I forgot.' Indeed, he had eaten most of it. But there was a little left at the very bottom of the jar . . .

March 14

. . . Winnie-the-Pooh
had been trying to get the
honey-jar off his head.
The more he shook it,
the more tightly it stuck.
'Bother!' he said, inside the jar,
and, *'Oh, help!'*
and, mostly, *'Ow!'*

March 15

'Heff,' said Piglet, breathing so hard that he could hardly speak, 'a Heff – a Heff – a Heffalump.'

'Where?'

March 16

'There!' said Piglet. 'Isn't it *awful?*'
And he held on tight to Christopher Robin's hand.
Suddenly Christopher Robin began to laugh ...
And while he was still laughing – *Crash* went
the Heffalump's head against the tree-root,
Smash went the jar, and out
came Pooh's head again ...

March 17

'Oh, Bear!' said Christopher
Robin. 'How I do love you!'
'So do I,' said Pooh.

March 18

'Roo's fallen in!' cried Rabbit, and he and
Christopher Robin came rushing down to the rescue.
'Look at me swimming!' squeaked Roo from the middle of his pool,
and was hurried down a waterfall into the next pool.

March 19

Eeyore had turned round
and hung his tail over
the first pool . . . grumbling
quietly to himself,
and saying, 'All this washing;
but catch on to my tail,
little Roo, and you'll
be all right.'

March 20

Eeyore was sitting with his tail in the water
when they all got back to him.
'Tell Roo to be quick, somebody,' he said.
'My tail's getting cold. I don't want to mention it, but I just mention it.
I don't want to complain, but there it is. My tail's cold.'

'A tail isn't
a tail to *them*, it's just
a Little Bit Extra at the back.'

March 22

'As I expected,' he said. 'Lost all feeling.
Numbed it. That's what it's done. Numbed it.
Well, as long as nobody minds,
I suppose it's all right.'

March 23

Here is Edward Bear, coming downstairs now, bump, bump, bump, on the back of his head, behind Christopher Robin. It is, as far as he knows, the only way of coming downstairs . . .

March 24

. . . but sometimes he feels
that there really is another way,
if only he could stop bumping for a
moment and think of it. And then he feels
that perhaps there isn't. Anyhow, here he is at
the bottom, and ready to be introduced to you.
Winnie-the-Pooh.

March 25

'Piglet,' said Rabbit, taking out
a pencil, and licking the end of it,
'you haven't any pluck.'
'It is hard to be brave,' said Piglet,
sniffing slightly, 'when you're only
a Very Small Animal.'

March 26

'You mean Piglet.
The little fellow with
the excited ears.
That's Piglet.'

March 27

What was a Heffalump like?

Was it Fierce?

Did it come when you whistled? And *how* did it come?

Was it Fond of Pigs at all?

March 28

And then he had a Clever Idea.
He would go up very quietly to the Six Pine
Trees now, peep very cautiously into the Trap,
and see if there *was* a Heffalump there.
And if there was, he would go back to bed,
and if there wasn't, he wouldn't.

'Help, help!' cried Piglet.
'A Heffalump, a Horrible Heffalump!'

March 30

'It's a little Anxious,'
he said to himself,
'to be a Very Small
Animal Entirely
Surrounded
by Water.'

March 31

Then suddenly he remembered a story
which Christopher Robin had told him about
a man on a desert island who had written
something in a bottle and
thrown it into the sea . . .

April 1

And he wrote on one side of the paper:
HELP!
PIGLIT (ME)
and on the other side:
IT'S ME PIGLIT, HELP HELP!

April 2

Then he put the paper in the bottle . . . and leant out of his window as far as he could lean without falling in, and he threw the bottle as far as he could throw – *splash*!

April 3

. . . he watched it floating slowly away in the distance . . . and then suddenly he knew that he would never see it again and that he had done all that he could do to save himself.

April 4

And then he gave a very long sigh and said, 'I wish Pooh were here. It's so much more friendly with two.'

April 5

'This is Serious,' said Pooh. 'I must have an Escape.'
So he took his largest pot of honey and
escaped with it to a broad branch of his tree . . .

April 6

He said to himself: 'If a bottle can float,
then a jar can float, and if a jar floats, I can sit
on the top of it, if it's a very big jar.'

April 7

So he took his biggest jar, and corked it up.
'All boats have to have a name,' he said,
'so I shall call mine *The Floating Bear*.'

April 8

For a little while Pooh and *The Floating Bear* were uncertain as to which of them was meant to be on the top, but after trying one or two different positions, they settled down with *The Floating Bear* underneath and Pooh triumphantly astride it . . .

April 9

'Now then, Pooh,' said Christopher Robin,
'where's your boat?'

April 10

'Sometimes it's a Boat, and sometimes
it's more of an Accident. It all depends.'
'Depends on what?'
'On whether I'm on the top of it or underneath it.'

April 11

Pooh got in.
He was just
beginning to say
that it was all right
now, when he found
that it wasn't, so after
a short drink . . .
he waded back to
Christopher Robin.

April 12

You can imagine
Piglet's joy when at
last the ship came
in sight of him.
In after-years he
liked to think that he
had been in Very Great
Danger during the
Terrible Flood . . .

April 13

'3 Cheers
for Pooh!
(For who?)
For Pooh —
(Why what did he do?)
I thought you knew;
He saved his friend from a wetting!
3 Cheers for Bear!
(For where?)
For Bear —

April 14

'He couldn't swim,
But he rescued him!
(He rescued who?)
Oh, listen, do!
I am talking of Pooh –
(Of who?)
Of Pooh!
(I'm sorry I keep forgetting).

April 15

'Well, Pooh was a Bear of Enormous Brain —
(Just say it again!)
Of enormous brain —
(Of enormous what?)
Well, he ate a lot,
And I don't know if he could swim or not,
But he managed to float
On a sort of boat
(On a sort of what?)
Well, a sort of pot —

April 16

'So now let's give him three hearty cheers
(So now let's give him three hearty whiches)
And hope he'll be with us for years and years,
And grow in health and wisdom and riches!

April 17

'3 Cheers for Pooh!
(For who?)
For Pooh –
3 Cheers for Bear!
(For where?)
For Bear –
3 Cheers for the wonderful
Winnie-the-Pooh!
(Just tell me, somebody – WHAT DID HE DO?*)*'

April 18

'Good morning, Eeyore,' said Pooh.

'Good morning, Pooh Bear,' said Eeyore gloomily.

'If it is a good morning,' he said.

'Which I doubt,' said he.

April 19

'When you wake up in the morning, Pooh,'
said Piglet at last, 'what's the first thing
you say to yourself?'
'What's for breakfast?' said Pooh.
'What do *you* say, Piglet?'
'I say, I wonder what's going to happen
exciting *to-day*?' said Piglet.
Pooh nodded thoughtfully.
'It's the same thing,' he said.

April 20

At breakfast that morning (a simple meal of
marmalade spread lightly over a honeycomb or two)
he had suddenly thought of a new song.

April 21

'Sing Ho!
for the life of a Bear!
Sing Ho! for the life of a Bear!
I don't much mind if it rains or snows,
'Cos I've got a lot of honey
on my nice new nose!

April 22

'I don't much care if it snows or thaws,
'Cos I've got a lot of honey on my nice clean paws!
Sing Ho! for a Bear!
Sing Ho! for a Pooh!
And I'll have a little something in an hour or two!'

April 23

'Pooh,' said Rabbit kindly,
  'you haven't any brain.'
'I know,' said Pooh humbly.

April 24

'I remember my uncle saying
once that he had seen cheese
just this colour.' So he put his
tongue in, and took a large lick.
'Yes,' he said, 'it is. No doubt
about that. And honey,
I should say, right down to the bottom of
the jar. Unless, of course,' he said,
'somebody put cheese in at the bottom
just for a joke.'

April 25

Pooh was sitting in his house one day,
counting his pots of honey, when there
came a knock on the door.
'Fourteen,' said Pooh. 'Come in.
Fourteen. Or was it fifteen? Bother.
That's muddled me.'

April 26

'If there's a
buzzing-noise, somebody's
making a buzzing-noise,
and the only reason for making
a buzzing-noise that *I* know
of is because you're
a bee.'

April 27

Then he thought
another long time, and said:
'And the only reason for being a bee
that I know of is making honey.'
And then he got up, and said:
'And the only reason for
making honey is so
as *I* can eat it.'

April 28

So he began to climb the tree. He climbed and he climbed and he climbed, and as he climbed he sang a little song to himself.

April 29

It went like this:
'Isn't it funny
How a bear likes honey?
Buzz! Buzz! Buzz!
I wonder why he does?'

April 30

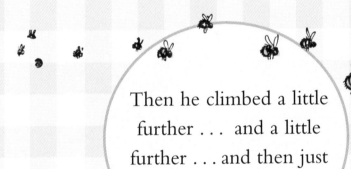

Then he climbed a little
further ... and a little
further ... and then just
a little further.

May 1

Crack!

'Oh, help!' said Pooh, as he
dropped ten feet on to the
branch below him . . .
'It all comes, I suppose,'
he decided, as he said
good-bye to the last branch,
spun round three times,
and flew gracefully into a
gorse-bush, 'it all comes of
liking honey so much.'

May 2

He crawled out of the gorse-bush,
brushed the prickles from his nose,
and began to think again. And the first person
he thought of was Christopher Robin.

May 3

'Good morning,
Christopher Robin,'
he said.
'Good morning,
Winnie-*ther*-Pooh,'
said you.
'I wonder if you've got
such a thing as a balloon
about you?'

May 4

Winnie-the-Pooh
looked round to
see that nobody was
listening, put his paw
to his mouth, and said
in a deep whisper:
'*Honey!*'
'But you don't get honey
with balloons!'
'*I* do,' said Pooh.

May 5

'Wouldn't they notice *you* underneath
the balloon?' you asked.
'They might or they might not,'
said Winnie-the-Pooh.
'You never can tell with bees.'

May 6

He thought for a moment and said: 'I shall
try to look like a small black cloud.
That will deceive them.'
'Then you had better have
the blue balloon,'
you said; and so it was decided.

May 7

'What do I look like?'
'You look like a Bear holding
on to a balloon,'
you said.
'Not,' said Pooh anxiously,
'– not like a small black cloud
in a blue sky?'

May 8

'Not very much.'
'Ah, well, perhaps
from up here it looks
different. And, as I say,
you never can tell
with bees.'

May 9

'Christopher Robin!' he said in a loud whisper.
'Hallo!'
'I think the bees *suspect* something!'
'What sort of thing?'
'I don't know. But something tells me that they're *suspicious!*'

May 10

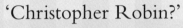

'Christopher Robin?'
'Yes?'
'Have you an
umbrella in
your house?'
'I think so.'

May 11

'I wish you would bring it out here, and walk up and down with it, and look up at me every now and then, and say "Tut-tut, it looks like rain." I think, if you did that, it would help with the deception which we are practising on these bees.'

May 12

'How sweet to be a Cloud
Floating in the Blue!
Every little cloud
Always sings aloud.'

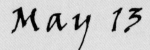

May 13

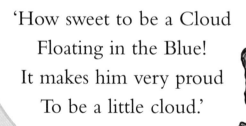

'How sweet to be a Cloud
Floating in the Blue!
It makes him very proud
To be a little cloud.'

May 14

'Christopher Robin, you must shoot
the balloon with your gun.
Have you got your gun?'
'Of course I have,' you said.
'But if I do that, it will spoil the balloon,' you said.
'But if you *don't*,' said Pooh,
'I shall have to let go,
and that would spoil *me*.'

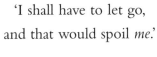

May 15

A bear, however hard he tries,
Grows tubby without exercise.
Our Teddy Bear is short and fat,
Which is not to be wondered at . . .

May 16

'He gets what
exercise he can
By falling off
the ottoman,
But generally
seems to lack
The energy to
clamber back.

May 17

'Now tubbiness is just the thing
Which gets a fellow wondering;
And Teddy worried lots about
The fact that he was rather stout.'

May 18

'Nearly eleven o'clock,' said Pooh happily. 'You're just in time for a little smackerel of something . . .'

May 19

It was a warm day, and he
had a long way to go.
He hadn't gone more than half-way
when a sort of funny feeling
began to creep all over him . . .
It was just as if somebody
inside him were saying,
'Now then, Pooh,
time for a little
something.'

May 20

Pooh knew
what he meant,
but, being a Bear of
Very Little Brain,
couldn't think
of the words.

May 21

[Piglet] felt so
Foolish and Uncomfortable
that he had almost decided
to run away to Sea
and be a Sailor . . .

May 22

'Look in my cupboard, Tigger dear, and see
what you'd like.' Because she knew at once
that, however big Tigger seemed to be,
he wanted as much kindness as Roo.

May 23

'I am a Bear of Very Little Brain,
and long words Bother me.'

May 24

'Yes, those are dragons all right,' said Pooh.
'As soon as I saw their beaks I knew.'

May 25

'That's right,' said Eeyore. 'Sing. Umty-tiddly, umty-too.
Here we go gathering Nuts and May.
Enjoy yourself.'

May 26

'Ah!' said Rabbit, who never let things come to him, but always went and fetched them.

May 27

'I could spend a happy morning
Seeing Roo,
I could spend a happy morning
Being Pooh.

May 28

'For it doesn't seem to matter,
If I don't get any fatter
(And I *don't* get any fatter),
What I do.'

May 29

He looked
up at his clock,
which had stopped
at five minutes to
eleven some
weeks ago.

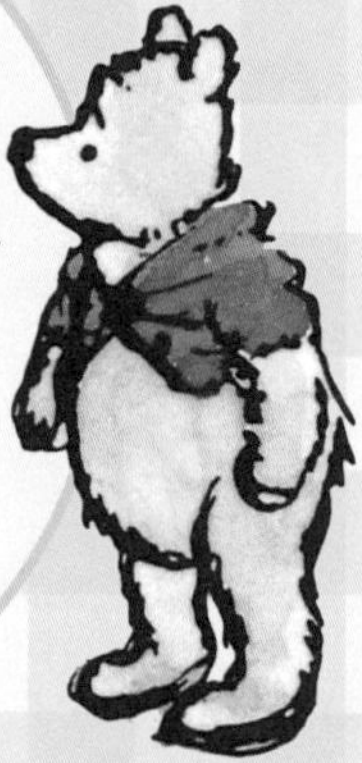

May 30

'They're funny things, Accidents.
You never have them till you're
having them.'

May 31

One day, when Pooh was walking towards this bridge,
he was trying to make up a piece of poetry
about fir-cones because . . . he felt singy.

June 1

He had just come to the bridge; and not looking
where he was going, he tripped over something, and
the fir-cone jerked out of his paw into the river.
'Bother,' said Pooh, as it floated slowly under
the bridge, and he went back to get another . . .

June 2

'That's funny,' said Pooh. 'I dropped it on the other side,' said Pooh, 'and it came out on this side! I wonder if it would do it again?' And he went back for some more fir-cones.

June 3

It did.
It kept on doing it . . .
And that was the
beginning of the game
called Poohsticks . . .
But they played with
sticks instead of fir-cones,
because they were
easier to mark.

June 4

Roo fell in twice,
the first time by accident
and the second time on
purpose, because he
suddenly saw Kanga
coming from the Forest,
and he knew he'd have
to go to bed anyhow.

June 5

Tigger and Eeyore went off together,
because Eeyore wanted to tell Tigger How
to Win at Poohsticks, which you do by letting
your stick drop in a twitchy sort of way.

June 6

'I can see mine!' cried Roo. 'No, I can't, it's something else.

Can you see yours, Piglet? . . .

There it is! No, it isn't.'

June 7

'I expect my stick's stuck,'
said Roo.
'Rabbit, my stick's stuck.
Is your stick stuck, Piglet?'
'They always take longer
than you think,' said Rabbit.
'How long do you *think*
they'll take?' asked Roo.

June 8

'Are you *sure* it's mine?' squeaked Piglet excitedly.

'Yes, because it's grey. A big grey one.

Here it comes! A very – big – grey –

Oh, no, it isn't, it's Eeyore.'

And out floated Eeyore.

June 9

'I've got a sort of idea,'
said Pooh at last,
'but I don't suppose it's a very good one.'
'I don't suppose it is either,' said Eeyore.

June 10

'*Now!*' said Rabbit.
Pooh dropped his stone.
There was a loud splash,
and Eeyore disappeared . . .

June 11

It was an anxious
moment for
the watchers on the
bridge. They looked
. . . and looked.

June 12

'Oh, Eeyore, you *are* wet!' said Piglet, feeling him.
Eeyore shook himself, and asked somebody to explain
to Piglet what happened when you had been
inside a river for quite a long time.

June 13

'Oo,' said Roo excitedly, 'did somebody push you?'
'Somebody BOUNCED me. I was just thinking
by the side of the river . . . when I received
a loud BOUNCE.'

June 14

'I didn't really.
I had a cough, and
I happened to be behind Eeyore,
and I said,
"*Grrrr-oppp-ptschschschz.*"'

June 15

'Friends,' he said, 'including oddments, it is a
great pleasure, or perhaps I had better say it has
been a great pleasure so far, to see you at my party.'

June 16

'A little
Consideration,
a little Thought
for Others,
makes all the
difference.'

'Rabbit's clever,'
said Pooh thoughtfully.
'Yes,' said Piglet, 'Rabbit's clever.'
. . . 'I suppose,' said Pooh,
'that that's why he never
understands anything.'

June 18

'Oh, the honey-bees are gumming
On their little wings, and humming
That the summer, which is coming,
Will be fun.

June 19

'And the cows are almost cooing,
And the turtle-doves are mooing,
Which is why a Pooh is poohing
In the sun.'

June 20

'Hallo, Rabbit,'
said Pooh dreamily.
'Did you make that song up?'
'Well, I sort of made it up,'
said Pooh. 'It isn't Brain,'
he went on humbly, 'because
You Know Why, Rabbit;
but it comes to me
sometimes.'

June 21

Piglet thought that they ought to have a
Reason for going to see everybody . . .
if Pooh could think of something.

June 22

Pooh could.
'We'll go because it's Thursday,' he said,
'and we'll go to wish everybody a
Very Happy Thursday. Come on, Piglet.'

June 23

'Hallo, Piglet,' he said. 'I thought you were out.'
'No,' said Piglet, 'it's you who were out, Pooh.'
'So it was,' said Pooh. 'I knew one of us was.'

June 24

...although Eating Honey
was a very good thing to do,
there was a moment just
before you began to eat it
which was better than when
you were ...

June 25

Christopher Robin was going away. Nobody knew
why he was going; nobody knew where he was
going; indeed, nobody even knew why
he knew that Christopher Robin
was going away.

June 26

'... what I like *doing* best is Nothing,'
said Christopher Robin.
'How do you do Nothing?'
asked Pooh, after he had
wondered for a long time.

June 27

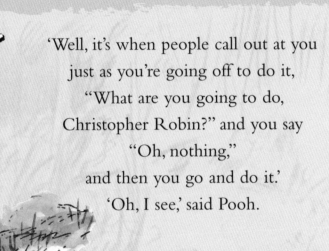

'Well, it's when people call out at you
just as you're going off to do it,
"What are you going to do,
Christopher Robin?" and you say
"Oh, nothing,"
and then you go and do it.'
'Oh, I see,' said Pooh.

June 28

'Is it a very Grand thing
to be an Afternoon,
what you said?'
'A what?' said Christopher Robin . . .
'On a horse?' explained Pooh.
'A Knight?'. . .
'Could a Bear be one?'

June 29

'Of course he could!' said Christopher
Robin. 'I'll make you one.' And he
took a stick and touched Pooh
on the shoulder, and said,
'Rise, Sir Pooh de Bear,
most faithful of all my Knights.'

June 30

'Here – we – are,'
said Rabbit very slowly and
carefully, 'all – of – us, and
then, suddenly . . . We find
a Strange Animal among us.
An animal of whom we had
never even heard before!
An animal who carries her
family about with her
in her pocket!'

July 1

'Suppose *I* carried *my* family about
with me in my pocket,
how many pockets should I want?'
'Sixteen,' said Piglet.
'Seventeen, isn't it?' said Rabbit.
'And one more for a handkerchief –
that's eighteen.
Eighteen pockets in one suit!'

July 2

'There's just one thing,' said Piglet, fidgeting a bit.
'I was talking to Christopher Robin, and he said that a Kanga was
Generally Regarded as One of the Fiercer Animals.'

July 3

'Now listen all of you,' said Rabbit
when he had finished writing,
and Pooh and Piglet sat listening very eagerly
with their mouths open.

July 4

This was what Rabbit read out:

PLAN TO CAPTURE
BABY ROO

1. *General Remarks*. Kanga runs faster than
any of Us, even Me.

2. *More General Remarks*. Kanga never takes her
eyes off Baby Roo, except when he's safely
buttoned up in her pocket.

July 5

3. *Therefore.* If we are to capture
Baby Roo, we must get a Long Start,
because Kanga runs faster than any of Us,
even Me. *(See 1.)*

4. *A Thought.* If Roo had jumped out of Kanga's
pocket and Piglet had jumped in,
Kanga wouldn't know the difference,
because Piglet is a Very Small Animal.

5. Like Roo.

July 6

6. But Kanga would have to be looking the other way first, so as not to see Piglet jumping in.

7. *(See 2.)*

8. *Another Thought.* But if Pooh was talking to her very excitedly, she might look the other way for a moment.

9. And then I could run away with Roo.

10. Quickly.

11. *And Kanga wouldn't discover*
   the difference
   until Afterwards.

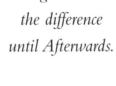

July 8

Piglet was so excited at the idea of being Useful that he forgot to be frightened any more, and when Rabbit went on to say that Kangas were only Fierce during the winter months, being at other times of an Affectionate Disposition, he could hardly sit still . . .

July 9

Rabbit said in a loud voice 'In you go, Roo!'
and in jumped Piglet, into Kanga's pocket,
and off scampered Rabbit, with Roo in his paws,
as fast as he could.

July 10

Of course as soon as Kanga unbuttoned her pocket,
she saw what had happened.

July 11

'I am not at all sure,' said Kanga in a thoughtful voice,
'that it wouldn't be a good idea to have a *cold* bath
this evening. Would you like that, Roo, dear?'

July 12

'*Ow!*' cried Piglet.
'Let me out! I'm Piglet!'
'Don't open the mouth, dear,
or the soap goes in,' said Kanga.
'There! What did I tell you?'

July 13

Never had Henry Pootel Piglet run so fast as he ran then,
and he didn't stop running until he had got quite close
to his house. But when he was a hundred yards away
he stopped running, and rolled the rest of the way home . . .

July 14

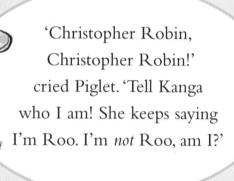

'Christopher Robin, Christopher Robin!' cried Piglet. 'Tell Kanga who I am! She keeps saying I'm Roo. I'm *not* Roo, am I?'

July 15

'I knew it
wasn't Piglet,' said Kanga.
'I wonder who it can be.'
'Perhaps it's some relation of
Pooh's,' said Christopher
Robin . . . 'I shall call
it Pootel.'

July 16

'Christopher Robin
depends on Me. He's fond of Pooh
and Piglet and Eeyore, and so am I,
but they haven't any Brain.
Not to notice.'

July 17

'You can go and collect some fir-cones for me,'
said Kanga, giving them a basket.
So they went to the Six Pine Trees, and threw
fir-cones at each other until they had forgotten
what they came for . . .

July 18

'. . . there are twelve pots of honey in my cupboard,
and they've been calling to me for hours.'

July 19

... until suddenly he found
himself at his own front door again.
And it was eleven o'clock.
Which was Time-for-a-
little-something ...

July 20

'Hallo, Piglet,' said Pooh.
'Hallo, Pooh,' said Piglet . . .
'I'm planting a haycorn, Pooh, so that it can grow
up into an oak-tree, and have lots of haycorns
just outside the front door instead of having to
walk miles and miles, do you see, Pooh?'

July 21

'Well,' said Pooh, 'if I plant a
honeycomb outside my house,
then it will grow up into a beehive.'
Piglet wasn't quite sure about this.

July 22

'Or a *piece* of a honeycomb,' said Pooh, 'so as not to waste too much.'

July 23

'Pooh, it's a very difficult thing, planting,
unless you know how to do it,' he said;
and he put the acorn in the hole he had made,
and covered it up with earth, and jumped on it.

July 24

'I do know,' said Pooh,
'because Christopher Robin gave me a
mastershalum seed, and I planted it, and I'm going
to have mastershalums all over the front door.'
'I thought they were called nasturtiums,'
said Piglet . . .

July 25

'Cottleston, Cottleston, Cottleston Pie,
A fish can't whistle and neither can I.
Ask me a riddle and I reply:
"Cottleston, Cottleston, Cottleston Pie."'

July 26

'Is that the end of the story?' asked Christopher Robin.

'That's the end of that one. There are others.'

'About Pooh and Me?'

'And Piglet and Rabbit and all of you.'

July 27

She had sent them out with a packet of
watercress sandwiches for Roo and a packet of
extract–of–malt sandwiches for Tigger . . .

July 28

Piglet took Pooh's arm, in case Pooh was frightened.

'Is it One of the Fiercer Animals?' he said,

looking the other way.

Pooh nodded.

'It's a Jagular,' he said.

'Pooh!' he cried. 'I believe it's Tigger and Roo!'
'So it is,' said Pooh. 'I thought it was a Jagular
and another Jagular.'

July 30

'Tiggers can't climb downwards, because their tails get in the way,
only upwards, and Tigger forgot about that when we started,
and he's only just remembered.'

July 31

'Ow!' he shouted as the tree flew past him. 'Look out!' cried Christopher Robin to the others.

August 1

'Tigger is all right, *really*,' said Piglet lazily.
'Of course he is,' said Christopher Robin.

August 2

'I just like to know,' said Pooh humbly.'
So as I can say to myself: "I've got
fourteen pots of honey left."
Or fifteen, as the case may be.
It's sort of comforting.'

August 3

...they came to
an enchanted place
on the very top of
the Forest called
Galleons Lap,
which is sixty-
something trees
in a circle ...

August 4

It was a drowsy summer afternoon, and the Forest was
full of gentle sounds, which all seemed to be saying
to Pooh, 'Don't listen to Rabbit, listen to me.'

August 5

'I'll come and watch you,' said Christopher
Robin. So he went home with Pooh,
and watched him for quite a long time . . .

August 6

'Many happy returns
of the day,' called out
Pooh, forgetting that
he had said it already.
'Thank you, Pooh,
I'm having them,' said
Eeyore gloomily.

August 7

Pooh sat down on
a large stone, and tried
to think this out. It sounded
to him like a riddle, and
he was never much good
at riddles, being a Bear
of Very Little Brain.

August 8

... he was doing his Stoutness
Exercises in front of the glass:
Tra-la-la, tra-la-la,
as he stretched up as high
as he could go, and then
Tra-la-la, tra-la – oh, help! – la,
as he tried to reach his toes.

August 9

'Pooh,' said Piglet
reproachfully, 'haven't you
been listening to what
Rabbit was saying?'
'I listened, but I had a small
piece of fluff in my ear.
Could you say it again,
please, Rabbit?'

August 10

'This
warm and
sunny Spot
Belongs to Pooh.
And here he
wonders what
He's going
to do.'

August 11

The sun was so delightfully warm . . . that Pooh had almost
decided to go on being Pooh in the middle of the stream
for the rest of the morning.

August 12

'It's just the place,'
he explained,
'for an Ambush.'
'What sort of bush?'
whispered
Pooh to Piglet.

August 13

'An ambush,' said Owl,
  'is a sort of Surprise.'
    'So is a gorse-bush
sometimes,' said Pooh.

August 14

'We are not *talking* about gorse-bushes,'
said Owl a little crossly.
'I am,' said Pooh.

August 15

'It's – I wondered – It's only – Rabbit, I suppose *you*
don't know. What does the North Pole *look* like?'
'Well,' said Rabbit, stroking his whiskers,
'now you're asking me.'

August 16

'Pooh's found the North Pole,' said Christopher Robin. 'Isn't that lovely?' Pooh looked modestly down.

August 17

Owl was telling Kanga
an Interesting Anecdote full of
long words like Encyclopaedia and
Rhododendron to which Kanga wasn't listening.

August 18

'. . . because you can't help respecting anybody who can
spell TUESDAY, even if he doesn't spell it right;
but spelling isn't everything.'

August 19

'You'll like Owl.
He flew past a day or two ago
and noticed me. He didn't actually say
anything, mind you, but he knew it was me.'

August 20

'Rabbit,' said Pooh to himself. 'I *like* talking to Rabbit . . .
He uses short, easy words, like, "What about lunch?"
and, "Help yourself, Pooh."'

August 21

'Done what to it?'
said Pooh.
'Organized it.
Which means – well, it's
what you do to a Search,
when you don't all look
in the same place at once.'

August 22

'Is Piglet organdized too?'
'We all are,' said Rabbit, and off he went.

August 23

Eeyore swished his tail . . . and said,
'Everybody crowds round so in this Forest.
There's no Space. I never saw a more Spreading lot
of animals in my life, and in all the wrong places.'

August 24

'Do go and see, Owl.
Because Pooh hasn't got
very much brain, and he
might do something silly,
and I do love him so, Owl.'

August 25

'Let's look for dragons,' I said to Pooh.
'Yes, let's,' said Pooh to Me.
We crossed the river and found a few –
'Yes, those are dragons all right,' said Pooh . . .

August 26

'Let's frighten the dragons,' I said to Pooh.
'That's right,' said Pooh to Me.
'*I'm* not afraid,' I said to Pooh,
And I held his hand and I shouted,
'Shoo!'

August 27

[Piglet's] grandfather had had two names
in case he lost one – Trespassers after an
uncle, and William after Trespassers.

August 28

Piglet comes in for a
good many things which
Pooh misses; because you
can't take Pooh to school
without everybody knowing
it, but Piglet is so small that
he slips into a pocket . . .

August 29

'Hallo, Eeyore!' said Roo.
Eeyore nodded gloomily at him.
'It will rain soon, you see if it doesn't,' he said.

August 30

'Without Pooh,' said Rabbit solemnly . . .
'the adventure would be impossible.'

August 31

'You seem so sad, Eeyore.'
'Sad? Why should I be sad?
It's my birthday.
The happiest day of the year.'

September 1

This was too much
for Pooh ... he felt that he
must get poor Eeyore a present of
some sort at once, and he could
always think of a proper
one afterwards.

September 2

'I'm giving him a Useful Pot to Keep Things In,
and I wanted to ask you –'...
'You ought to write "*A Happy Birthday*" on it.'
'*That* was what I wanted to ask you,' said Pooh.
'Because my spelling is Wobbly. It's good spelling
but it Wobbles, and the letters get in the
wrong places.'

September 3

So Owl wrote . . .
HIPY PAPY BTHUTHDTH
THUTHDA BTHUTHDY
Pooh looked on admiringly.
'I'm just saying
"A Happy Birthday",'
said Owl carelessly.

September 4

'Many happy returns of the day,'
called out Pooh, forgetting that he
had said it already.
'Thank you, Pooh, I'm having them,'
said Eeyore gloomily.

September 5

. . . Piglet had gone back
to his own house to get
Eeyore's balloon . . .
he didn't look where he
was going . . . and suddenly
he put his foot in a
rabbit hole, and fell down
flat on his face.

September 6

BANG!!!???★★★!!!

Piglet lay there, wondering what had happened.

September 7

'. . . I – I – oh, Eeyore, I burst the balloon!' . . .

'My birthday balloon?'

'Yes, Eeyore,' said Piglet, sniffing a little.

September 8

'Here it is.
With – with many
happy returns of the day.'
And he gave Eeyore the
small piece of damp rag.
'Is this it?' said Eeyore,
a little surprised.

September 9

'It's a Useful Pot,' said Pooh. 'Here it is.
And it's got "A Very Happy Birthday
with love from Pooh" written on it.'

September 10

When Eeyore saw the pot, he became quite excited.
'Why!' he said. 'I believe my Balloon
will just go into that Pot!' . . .
'So it does!' said Piglet. 'And it comes out!'

September 11

But Eeyore wasn't listening. He was taking
the balloon out, and putting it back again,
as happy as could be . . .

September 12

'Half an hour,'
said Owl, settling
himself comfortably.
'That will just give me time
to finish that story I was
telling you about my
Uncle Robert . . .'
Pooh closed
his eyes.

September 13

When he saw Piglet sitting in his best arm-chair,
he could only stand there rubbing his head . . .

September 14

'Poetry and Hums
aren't things which
you get, they're things
which get *you*.
And all you can do
is to go where they
can find you.'

September 15

'It's a very funny thought that, if Bears were Bees,
They'd build their nests at the *bottom* of trees.
And that being so (if the Bees were Bears),
We shouldn't have to climb up all these stairs.'

September 16

'Hallo!' said Tigger, and he sounded so close suddenly that
Piglet would have jumped if Pooh hadn't accidentally
been sitting on most of him.

September 17

Rabbit nudged Pooh, and Pooh looked about for Piglet to nudge,
but couldn't find him, and Piglet went on breathing wet bracken
as quietly as he could, and felt very brave and excited.

September 18

'What's twice eleven?'
I said to Pooh,
('Twice what?' said Pooh
to Me.)
'I *think* it ought to
be twenty-two.'
'Just what I think myself,'
said Pooh.

September 19

'The rissolution,' said Rabbit,
'is that we all sign it,
and take it to Christopher Robin.'
So it was signed PooH, . . .

Pooh

September 20

. . . WOL, . . .

September 21

. . . PIGLIT, . . .

Piglit

September 22

. . . EOR, . . .

eOR

September 23

. . . RABBIT, . . .

Rabbit,

September 24

. . . KANGA, . . .

September 25

...BLOT,...

September 26

. . . SMUDGE, and they all went off to
Christopher Robin's house with it.

September 27

'Piglet, I have decided something.'
'What have you decided, Pooh?'
'I have decided to catch a Heffalump.'

September 28

It was going to be one of Rabbit's busy days.
As soon as he woke up he felt important,
as if everything depended upon him.

September 29

It was a Captainish sort of day, when
everybody said, 'Yes, Rabbit,' and, 'No, Rabbit,'
and waited until he had told them.

September 30

...it seemed hours
before he got them
into the shelter of the
Hundred Acre Wood...
to listen, a little nervously,
to the roaring of the gale
among the tree-tops.

October 1

'Supposing a tree fell down, Pooh,
when we were underneath it?'
'Supposing it didn't,' said Pooh, after careful thought.
Piglet was comforted by this . . .

October 2

Pooh's side of the room was slowly tilting upwards and his chair began sliding down on Piglet's. The clock slithered gently along the mantelpiece, collecting vases on the way . . .

October 3

In a corner of the room, the
table-cloth began to wriggle.
Then it wrapped itself into a
ball and rolled across the room.
Then it jumped up and
down once or twice,
and put out two ears.

October 4

'Pooh,'
said Piglet nervously.
'Yes?' said one of the chairs.
'Where are we?'
'I'm not quite sure,'
said the chair.

October 5

'Ah, Piglet,' said Owl, looking very much annoyed;
'where's Pooh?'
'I'm not quite sure,' said Pooh.

October 6

'Pooh,' said Owl severely,
'did *you* do that?'
'No,' said Pooh humbly.
'I don't *think* so.'

October 7

'I think it was the wind,'
said Piglet.
'I think your house has
blown down.'
'Oh, is that it? I thought
it was Pooh.'
'No,' said Pooh.

October 8

'If it was the wind,'
said Owl, considering
the matter, 'then it wasn't
Pooh's fault. No blame
can be attached to him.'
With these kind words
he flew up to look at
his new ceiling.

October 9

'. . . if we could get Piglet into the letter-box,
he might squeeze through the place
where the letters come, and climb
down the tree and run for help.'

October 10

Piglet said hurriedly that he had been getting bigger
lately ... and Owl said that he had had his letter-box
made bigger lately in case he got bigger letters,
so perhaps Piglet *might* ...

October 11

He squeezed and
he sqoze, and then
with one last squze
he was out.

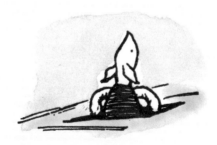

October 12

'It's all right,' he called
through the letter-box.
'Your tree is blown right
over, Owl . . .'

October 13

Here lies a tree which Owl (a bird)
Was fond of when it stood on end,
And Owl was talking to a friend
Called Me (in case you hadn't heard)
When something Oo occurred.

October 14

They had got a rope and were pulling Owl's chairs and pictures and things out of his old house . . .

Kanga was
. . . calling out to Owl,
'You won't want this dirty
old dish-cloth any more,
will you . . .?' and Owl was calling
back indignantly, 'Of course I do!
. . . it isn't a dish-cloth,
it's my shawl.'

October 16

'O gallant Piglet (PIGLET)! Ho!
Did Piglet tremble? Did he blinch?
No, no, he struggled inch by inch
Through LETTERS ONLY, as I know
Because I saw him go.'

October 17

'Oh!' said Piglet. 'Because I – I thought
I did blinch a little. Just at first. And it says,
"Did he blinch no no." That's why.'

October 18

'You only
blinched inside,'
said Pooh, 'and that's
the bravest way for a
Very Small Animal
not to blinch
that there is.'

October 19

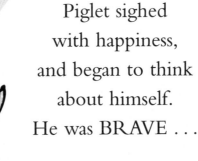

Piglet sighed
with happiness,
and began to think
about himself.
He was BRAVE . . .

October 20

'Don't mind Eeyore,' whispered Rabbit to Pooh. 'I told him all about it this morning.'

october 21

'All the Poetry in the Forest has been written by
Pooh, a Bear with a Pleasing Manner but a
Positively Startling Lack of Brain.'

October 22

These are my two drops of rain
Waiting on the window-pane.

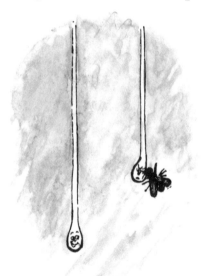

October 23

I am waiting
here to see
Which the
winning one
will be.

October 24

'Shall I look, too?'
said Pooh, who
was beginning to
feel a little eleven
o'clockish.

October 25

'You see, what I *meant* to do,' he explained, as he turned head-over-heels, and crashed on to another branch thirty feet below . . .

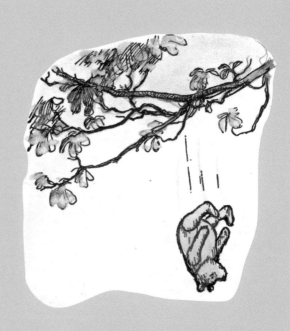

October 26

Once upon a time,
a very long time ago
now, about last Friday,
Winnie-the-Pooh lived in
a forest all by himself
under the name
of Sanders.

October 27

'Do you think you could very kindly lean against me,
'cos I keep pulling so hard that I fall over backwards.'

October 28

'Notice a meeting of everybody will meet at the
House at Pooh Corner to pass a Rissolution
By Order Keep to the Left
Signed Rabbit.'

October 29

'It's your fault, Eeyore.
You've never been to
see any of us.
You just stay here in
this one corner of the
Forest, waiting for the
others to come to you.
Why don't you go to
them sometimes?'

October 30

'Don't Bustle me,' said Eeyore,
getting up slowly.
'Don't now-then me.'

October 31

. . . when you are a Bear of Very Little Brain, and you Think of Things, you find sometimes that a Thing which seemed very Thingish inside you is quite different when it gets out into the open . . .

November 1

'The Poem which I am now about to read to you
was written by Eeyore, or Myself,
in a Quiet Moment.'

November 2

'Christopher Robin is going.
At least I think he is.
Where?
Nobody knows.
But he is going –
I mean he goes
(To rhyme with 'knows')

November 3

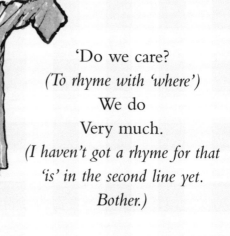

'Do we care?
(To rhyme with 'where')
We do
Very much.
*(I haven't got a rhyme for that
'is' in the second line yet.
Bother.)*

November 4

'The fact is this is more difficult
than I thought,
I ought –
(Very good indeed)

November 5

'*(Very awkward this,
it keeps going wrong.)*
Well, anyhow,
we send
Our love
END.'

November 6

'If anybody wants to clap,'
said Eeyore when he had read this,
'now is the time to do it.'

November 7

They all clapped.
'Thank you,' said Eeyore.
'Unexpected and gratifying,
if a little lacking in Smack.'

November 8

'It's much better than mine,'
said Pooh admiringly,
and he really thought it was.

November 9

'Well,' explained Eeyore modestly,
'it was meant to be.'

November 10

'Hush!' said Christopher Robin, turning round to Pooh, 'we're just coming to a Dangerous Place.'

November 11

If I were a bear,
And a big bear too,
I shouldn't much care
If it froze or snew;

November 12

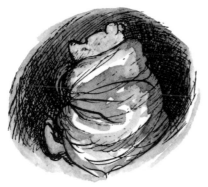

I shouldn't much mind
If it snowed or friz —
I'd be all fur-lined
With a coat like his!

November 13

. . . now I am Six, I'm as clever as clever.
So I think I'll be six now for ever and ever.

November 14

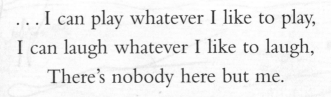

... I can play whatever I like to play,
I can laugh whatever I like to laugh,
There's nobody here but me.

November 15

It was a perfect morning for hurrying round to Pooh,
and saying, 'Very well, then, I'll tell Piglet . . .'

November 16

Rabbit came up importantly,
nodded to Piglet, and said,
'Ah, Eeyore,' in the voice of
one who would be saying
'Good-bye' in about
two more minutes.

November 17

'I don't hold with all this washing,' grumbled Eeyore. 'This modern Behind-the-ears nonsense.'

November 18

'The atmospheric conditions have been very
unfavourable lately,' said Owl.
'The what?'
'It has been raining,' explained Owl.

November 19

'What about a story?'
said Christopher Robin.
'*What* about a story?' I said.
'Could you very sweetly tell
Winnie-the-Pooh one?'
'I suppose I could,' I said. 'What
sort of stories does he like?'
'About himself. Because he's
that sort of Bear.'

November 20

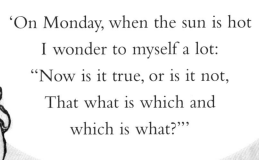

'On Monday, when the sun is hot
I wonder to myself a lot:
"Now is it true, or is it not,
That what is which and
which is what?"'

November 21

'On Tuesday,
when it hails and snows,
The feeling on me grows and grows
That hardly anybody knows
If those are these or
these are those.

November 22

'On Wednesday, when the sky is blue,
And I have nothing else to do,
I sometimes wonder if it's true
That who is what
and what is who.

November 23

'On Thursday, when it starts to freeze
And hoar-frost twinkles on the trees,
How very readily one sees
That these are whose –
but whose are these?

November 24

'On Friday –'
'Yes, it is, isn't it?' said Kanga,
not wanting to hear what happened on Friday.

November 25

Well, he was humming this hum to himself, and walking gaily along, wondering what everybody else was doing, and what it felt like, being somebody else, when suddenly he came to a sandy bank, and in the bank was a large hole.

November 26

Then he had an idea,
and I think that for a
Bear of Very Little Brain,
it was a good idea.

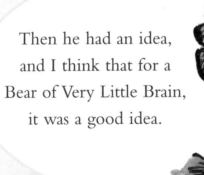

November 27

'It's all very well for Jumping Animals like Kangas,
but it's quite different for
Swimming Animals like Tiggers.'

November 28

'The flood-level has reached
an unprecedented height.'
'The who?'
'There's a lot of water about,'
explained Owl.

November 29

'And the cuckoo isn't cooing,
But he's cucking and he's ooing,
And a Pooh is simply poohing
Like a bird.'

November 30

The next moment the day became very bothering indeed,
because Pooh was so busy not looking where
he was going that he stepped on a piece of the Forest
which had been left out by mistake . . .

December 1

'What *I* think,' said Pooh, 'is I think we'll go to
Pooh Corner and see Eeyore, because perhaps his
house has been blown down . . .'

December 2

'Let's go and see *everybody*,' said Pooh.
'Because when you've been walking in the wind for miles,
and you suddenly go into somebody's house . . .
it's what I call a Friendly Day.'

December 3

Owl, wise though he was
in many ways, able to read
and write and spell his own
name WOL, yet somehow
went all to pieces over
delicate words like MEASLES
and BUTTEREDTOAST.

December 4

'It's Piglet!'
cried Pooh eagerly.
'Where are you?'
'Underneath,' said Piglet
in an underneath sort of way.
'Underneath what?'
'You,' squeaked Piglet.
'Get up!'

December 5

. . . when Piglet had sat down again, because he didn't know the wind was so strong, and had been helped up by Pooh, they started off.

December 6

There were Two little Bears who lived in a Wood,
And one of them was Bad and the other was Good.
Good Bear learnt his Twice Times One –
But Bad Bear left all his buttons undone.

December 7

'Has he written a letter saying
how much he enjoyed himself, and how
sorry he was he had to go suddenly?'
Christopher Robin didn't think he had.

December 8

'Tiggers never go on being Sad,' explained Rabbit.
'They get over it with Astonishing Rapidity.
I asked Owl, just to make sure, and he said that
that's what they always get over it with.'

December 9

I want a soldier
(A tall one, a red one),
I want a soldier who plays on the drum.

December 10

'I *didn't* sneeze.'
'Yes, you did, Owl.' . . .
'What I *said* was, "First *Issue* a Reward".'
'You're doing it again,' said Pooh sadly.

December 11

'But, Eeyore,' said Pooh in distress,
'what can we – I mean, how shall we – do you think if we –'
'Yes,' said Eeyore. 'One of those would be just the thing.
Thank you, Pooh.'

December 12

. . . Eeyore whispered back: 'I'm not saying there won't
be an Accident *now*, mind you. They're funny things,
Accidents. You never have them till you're having them.'

December 13

He hurried back
to his own house;
and his mind was so
busy on the way
with the hum that he
was getting ready
for Eeyore . . .

December 14

'And then we'll go out, Piglet,
and sing my song to Eeyore.'
'Which song, Pooh?'
'The one we're going to sing to Eeyore,' explained Pooh.

December 15

The wind had dropped, and the snow, tired of rushing round
in circles trying to catch itself up, now fluttered gently down
until it found a place on which to rest, and sometimes
the place was Pooh's nose and sometimes it wasn't . . .

December 16

Piglet was wearing a white muffler
round his neck and feeling more snowy
behind the ears than
he had ever felt before.

December 17

'Owl,' said Rabbit shortly, 'you and
I have brains. The others have fluff.
If there is any thinking to be done in
this Forest – and when I say thinking,
I mean thinking – you and I must do it.'

December 18

'. . . it's no good going home to practise it,
because it's a special Outdoor Song
which Has To Be Sung In The Snow.'

December 19

'The more it
SNOWS-tiddely-pom,
The more it
GOES-tiddely-pom
The more it
GOES-tiddely-pom
On
Snowing.

December 20

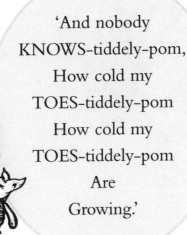

'And nobody
KNOWS-tiddely-pom,
How cold my
TOES-tiddely-pom
How cold my
TOES-tiddely-pom
Are
Growing.'

December 21

'Tiddely what?'
said Piglet.
'Pom,' said Pooh.
'I put that in to make
it more hummy.'

December 22

'And we will call this Pooh Corner. And we will build
an Eeyore House with sticks at Pooh Corner for Eeyore.'
'There was a heap of sticks on the other side
of the wood,' said Piglet.

December 23

'Thank you, Piglet,' said Pooh.
'What you have just said
will be a Great Help
to us, and because of it
I could call this place
Poohanpiglet Corner
if Pooh Corner didn't
sound better . . .'

December 24

'It just shows what can be done by taking a little trouble,' said Eeyore. 'Do you see, Pooh? Do you see, Piglet? Brains first and then Hard Work.'

December 25

'Hallo, Eeyore,' said Christopher Robin . . .
'It's snowing still,' said Eeyore gloomily . . .
'*And* freezing.'
'Is it?'
'Yes,' said Eeyore.

'However,' he said, brightening up a little,
'we haven't had an earthquake lately.'

December 26

'I don't know how it is, Christopher Robin,
but what with all this snow . . .
it isn't so Hot in my field about three o'clock
in the morning as some people think it is.'

December 27

'. . . but if it goes on snowing for another six weeks or so,
one of them will begin to say to himself:
"Eeyore can't be so very much too Hot about
three o'clock in the morning." And then it will Get About.
And they'll be Sorry.'

December 28

'*We've finished our HOUSE!*' sang the gruff voice.

'*Tiddely pom!*' sang the squeaky one.

'*It's a beautiful HOUSE . . .*'

'*Tiddely pom . . .*'

'*I wish it were MINE . . .*'

'*Tiddely pom . . .*'

December 29

... there was Eeyore's house, looking as comfy as anything. 'There you are,' said Piglet. 'Inside as well as outside,' said Pooh proudly.

December 30

Eeyore went inside
. . . and came out again.
'It's a remarkable thing,'
he said. 'It is my house,
and I built it where I said
I did, so the wind must have
blown it here . . . and here
it is as good as ever.
In fact, better in places.'
'Much better,' said Pooh
and Piglet together.

December 31

'Pooh, *promise* you won't forget about me, ever.
Not even when I'm a hundred.'
Pooh thought for a little. 'How old shall *I* be then?'
'Ninety-nine.'
Pooh nodded. 'I promise,' he said.